Big bully giants always seek
to scare and harm you.

WRITING CANVAS

WHAT GIANTS ARE TRYING TO SCARE YOU?
Write down anything that makes you feel afraid, small, or unsure.

TALK TO GOD ABOUT IT.
Tell Him what these giants are doing and ask HIM to fight for you.

SPEAK BACK TO THOSE BULLY GIANTS!!
Now write a bold message to those giants letting them know you are not afraid of them anymore.

HOW CAN YOU BE MORE OBEDIENT?

1.

2.

3.

4.

5.

6.

7.

LIST THE WAYS YOU ARE ALREADY OBEDIENT

1.

2.

3.

4.

5.

King Saul is tormented because of his continued disobedience.

WHAT WOULD YOU SAY TO ENCOURAGE AND UPLIFT SOMEONE WHO IS HURTING LIKE TAMAR IS HURTING?

Tamar is sad and very de-
pressed after her brother hurt her.
He was very wicked and selfish
when he mistreated her.

HOW CAN YOU SHOW KINDNESS TODAY? USE THIS PAGE AS A KINDNESS CANVAS ---DRAW, DOODLE OR CREATE ANYTHING THAT REMINDS YOU TO BE KIND.

USE THIS PRAYER CANVAS TO SHARE ANYTHING WITH GOD ---YOUR DREAMS, YOUR QUESTIONS, YOUR JOYS AND YOUR FEARS. WHETHER WITH WORDS OR PICTURES, GOD'S ALWAYS LISTENING AND READY TO HELP.

LOVE IS SOMETHING WE CAN SHOW EVERY DAY! USE THIS CANVAS TO DRAW OR WRITE ALL THE WAYS YOU CAN SHOW LOVE TO OTHERS.

Daniel was thrown in the lion's den but he was spared. They didn't even try to eat him.

THERE'S ALWAYS SOMETHING TO BE
THANKFUL FOR! USE THIS GRATITUDE CANVAS TO
DRAW OR WRITE THE BLESSINGS GOD HAS GIVEN TO
YOU---ANYTHING THAT MAKES YOUR HEART SMILE.

Haman was led by greed and power and a desire to hurt others.

HUMILITY MEANS THINKING OF OTHERS AND NOT NEEDING TO BE FIRST. USE THIS HUMILITY CANVAS TO DRAW OR WRITE WHAT IT LOOKS LIKE TO STAY KIND, CALM AND HUMBLE.

God made King Nebuchadnezzar crawl around on all fours for being arrogant and proud.

GOD FILLS OUR HEARTS AND THOUGHTS WITH BIG DREAMS AND BRIGHT IDEAS. USE THIS CANVAS TO CAPTURE WHAT INSPIRES YOU TO GROW, HOPE AND BELIEVE.

God spoke to Joseph in his dream and told him to leave Israel and take Mary and Baby Jesus to Egypt. This was so they could escape the wicked King Herod.

DID YOU KNOW WORDS HAVE THE POWER TO HURT OR TO HEAL?
ON THIS POETRY CANVAS, WRITE A POEM THAT SPEAKS LIFE,
BRINGS HOPE OR SPREADS KINDNESS. USE YOUR WORDS TO
BUILD, NOT BREAK.

Wicked King
Herod used his
power to hurt
many people.

HOW HAS OUR LORD AND SAVIOR HELPED YOU WITH A BULLYING SITUATION?

WHAT WOULD YOU DO TO ENCOURAGE SOMEONE WHO IS BEING BULLIED?

Our Lord and Savior Jesus Christ is our perfect
example against bullies and giants.

GOD MADE YOU STRONG, BRAVE AND VICTORIOUS! USE THIS CANVAS TO SHOW HOW YOU'VE OVERCOME CHALLENGES--- OR HOW YOU'RE TRUSTING GOD TO HELP YOU WIN YOUR BATTLES. DRAW, WRITE, OR CREATE YOUR VICTORY STORY!

God fights all our battles. When we call on Him,
He will smash enemies dow with HIS almighty
hand.

THIS COLORING BOOK IS BASED ON THE BOOK

VICTORIOUS! DEFEATING BULLIES AND GIANTS GOD'S WAY

BY DARNNELL REESE

ILLUSTRATED BY KEAGOE STITH
A NEW YORK BASED ARTIST @keagoe

www.ingramcontent.com/pod-product-compliance
Lightning Source LLC
Chambersburg PA
CBHW080905120626

46555CB00008B/2971